MY SOUL TO KEEP

A Collection of Life Stories and Resources in Preparation for Your Final Appointment

Dorene Benn Hudson

MY SOUL TO KEEP
A Collection of Life Stories and Resources in Preparation for Your Final Appointment

Copyright 2020@Dorene Benn Hudson

ISBN: 978-0-57-866798-0

Author: *Dorene Benn Hudson*
Editor: *Valerie L. McDowell*
Publisher: *Power2Excel*
Cover Design & Layout: *Faith Anne*
Photographer: *Aisha Butler of JazzyStudios*

ALL RIGHTS RESERVED

This book contains material protected under International and Federal Copyright Laws and Treaties. Any unauthorized reprint or use of this material is prohibited. No part of this book may be reproduced or transmitted in any form or by any means, electronic or mechanical, including photocopying, recording, or by any information storage and retrieval system without express written permission from the author at dbhudsonministries@gmail.com.

Printed and bound in the United States of America by IngramSpark

DEDICATION

All of who I am and who I hope to be in this earthly journey is credited to my Lord and Savior, Christ Jesus. I find that in this human tabernacle, where my soul dwells, I am completely inept, without the Holy Spirit of God to lead and guide me on this pilgrim path.

Throughout the writing of the manuscript I had been heavily challenged and have experienced many attacks by the enemy. This work was fiercely written and completed with God fighting for me and covering me. While under his wings, I trusted. Many nights I suffered greatly in pain, or met with frustration, or cried many tears, while also diligently caring for my dear ill husband. In addition, I had to navigate my own health challenges with regard to diabetes, vision issues, breast cancer issues, as well as my husband's prostate cancer concerns. Furthermore, my younger brother Milton was undergoing a bilateral lung transplant and was hospitalized for over a year, while our daughter in Delaware, Sharlene, became unexpectedly ill, and has now been an inpatient for the past seven months in several medical facilities. And then—my husband's recent diagnosis of b-cell lymphoma.

Whew...when I say "We are more than conquerors, and, we have the victory," know that this is the mantra we live, speak, and declare!

Along my journey God has afforded me relationships to make my life more complete in Him. To fulfill my portion of purposed work in His Kingdom, I acknowledge these great individuals as part of God's plan in my life.

Elder Sylvia Sewell
In you I have the treasure and true love of boundless family/friendship! Your endless travail of prayer and intercession for me and the family surpasses what is remarkable. Because of your love and devotion to our Mighty God, you are indeed His chosen vessel for such a time as this. Thank you for your tenacity of warring in the spirit and your labor of love as prayer warrior and intercessor for so many. I see endless jewels gracefully planted and flowing from your crown.

Dr. Brenda Pridgen
Our bond is a tried and true sisterhood. Over the course of our lives, you constantly helped me to see my worth and pushed me when I felt I had nothing to offer. Thank you for being my "gutsy" friend and always encouraging me to take the risks to defy the odds against us. To believe in myself and not listen to the naysayers, as we soared to become world-class agents of change. You are strong, magnificent, and soaring with power.

Diana E. Jones Ritter
Sister, you have stuck by my side and championed me through some of the worst blows and attacks, especially when the

enemy thought I was down and done with. You are my breast cancer survivor iconic example of living the best life. You were always there to help lift me back up and encourage me to keep riding on. You are indeed one of my true nurturers, always creating "fun times" for us to get away, relax, and regroup with a fresh new set of eyes! I am looking forward to our rocking chair and tea drinking days ahead.

C. Natasha Richburg
My manager friend for redevelopment, I thank you so much for taking time to speak clearly into my "head space," so that I could find my way back to re-focusing on evolving my business strategies and initiatives. I treasure the exciting times we experienced together as we engaged in the many festivities you created for launching new releases and establishing new artists. You make re-development exciting and worth the effort for so many.

Bishop Jason Nelson
Over 10 years ago between the years of 2008-09, a young minister began leading a church known as Greater Bethlehem Temple (GBT) in Randallstown, MD. Today, he is truly a great anointed vessel in God, and is known in the Kingdom for preaching a "rhema Word" as well as being an established national gospel recording artist. During those early years when we worked side by side in ministry efforts for the church, Bishop Jason saw in me what I was not acknowledging in myself. The Spirit of God had you to appoint and choose me as an elder of the church and to lead community outreach efforts for GBT as well as assist in administrative functions.

In addition, you later appointed me as lead for the Prayer Ministry of the GBT Tabernacle. As I worked in these capacities for the Lord, I was able to serve and effectively use my designated gifts for the assignments of caring for people who were in need of counsel, encouragement, were in heavy bereavement, were in states of hopelessness and despair, and who desired prayer and deliverance. I appreciate and thank you for respecting the gifts in me and allowing me to operate in them for the advancement of God's Kingdom.

Mia Redrick

Chief Giant and Coach Strategist! Your meals are indescribably delicious with all that you serve to us. As your fellow Giant protégés, we always hunger for more of the food you keep offering to us on business and strategy! I thank God for allowing our paths to connect at the right time and season of my life. You have given to me a new lens that clearly enabled me to envision and acknowledge more of the worth and value in myself. You have caused me to effectively leverage what I know, through changing former mindsets, becoming an action taker, and accurately positioning myself! I am grateful to you coach Mia, Love you much!

Valerie McDowell

I literally would not be here at this point in my life without YOU! You are the Sister Giant, my kick-butt Book Coach, Supporter, Encourager, Prayer warrior friend, and focus keeper. All I thought of accomplishing was only a constant dream until God planted you in my space and time. You understood this season of my life (with all its challenges), and yet you still managed to help me stay close to deadline after deadline. Even when I slipped up and started speaking the language of defeat, you were not having it! You canceled my negative thinking at its root and declared, "YOU WILL FINISH AND COMPLETE THIS MANUSCRIPT." Your pushy, sharp, clever-witted directives ordered me and kept me on my toes. Even when not in conversation with you, I could hear Coach Val's high-pitched voice, admonishing me to get it done! You are the exceptional Coach Excel-erator. I love and thank you so much for the strictness and keeping me on task. I look forward to the next manuscript project with you.

Family, Friends, and Church Support Team

My loving, patient, dedicated, man of confidence, James B. Hudson. You are my confidant, my dream catcher, my friend, road and life partner. As you have always said, you and me together, is the best place for us to be. You have always been my sweet Idaho-HUD, sticking by my side as you faithfully promised to me so long ago. Thanks for being the rock I can lean on. Loving you never ends!

My sons, Joshua Holloman and Jamal Holloman, *consistently devoted*, diligent, and addressing *any* need their mom presented. I appreciate how you willingly give of your time and attention to me. You are two of the best and most dependable sons any mother could want!

My sister and brother-in-love, Pamela and Leon Williams, always there to support me and James non-stop for so many things. My Aunt Bert for her flow of wisdom, guidance, and counsel; My four reliable, supportive brothers, Mike, Peewee, Kevin, and Bill, always there to offer and give of your time, skill, advice, and resources to me and James. Also Kev and Stacy, thank you for your support with helping to get my James to cancer treatments. Baby Sis Sharia, thank you for your texts of love, and prayers. My daughter Zakiyya Holloman, thank you for taking time to text and check-in on me, and your Pop James. Much love and appreciation to our Brother & Sister, Larry and Diana Ritter, for regularly driving down from Schenectady, NY to check on James & me, surprising James for his birthday, and your constant attentiveness to our needs. Also, appreciation to Sharlene Hudson, Jamie Hudson, Margaret Hudson, and Kuhlena Hudson for always calling or texting to check on your Dad and me. Special acknowledgement to Sylwaivon and Franklin King for their love and encouragement.

To my faithful spiritual children, Tina and Carlos Lacy, you have been there with James and I through some tough trials and stuck right by our side as we faced them. We are grateful to you both and appreciate you more than you know. Also, my other spiritual children, Christopher and Erica Lay, Pastor Glen and Jacqueline Jones, your calls, texts, encouragement and especially the faithful anointed prayers you keep sending up on our behalf, are gratefully treasured. Thanks for the flow of love and for stopping by to check in on us. I must also give shout-outs of sincere appreciation to Mr. Garcia Davis and Mr. Bobby Jones, two of the greatest top-notch home improvement guys on this planet. You both have been faithful over the years to help keep the Hudson home running smoothly and proficiently.

Our Highway Christian Church and Pastor Dennis Carver and Lady Camille Carver, so grateful for your love and dedication toward us. I appreciate you, little sister Camille, for your consistent prodding and gentle pushes for me to write, write, write. To all of the beautiful Saints in our church family, for the mighty support, encouragement, visits, constant flow of gifts, meals, calls, prayers without ceasing, and the many different types of kindnesses and thoughtful ways shown during my breast cancer journey and victory, and now with my James and his battle to victory. Each one of you hold a dear place in our hearts. I also thank my sweet spiritual Mother, Evangelist Mary Johns, for always covering me, my husband, our children, and our grandchildren, in your daily prayers.

For all the above and more. My soul loves Jesus!

TABLE OF CONTENTS

Dedication _____ *i*

Foreword _____ *xi*

Introduction _____ *1*

Chapter 1: Processing The Unimaginable _____ *5*

Chapter 2: My Hero Takes Flight _____ *11*

Chapter 3: The Designer's Masterpiece _____ *19*

Chapter 4: Another Father To Me _____ *31*

Chapter 5: Church And Family Icon _____ *39*

Chapter 6: Gang Allegiances _____ *45*

Chapter 7: An Unexpected Death _____ *51*

Chapter 8: When A Lengthy Illness Arrives _____ *53*

Reflections _____ *59*

Final Thoughts _____ *65*

Epilogue _____ *69*

My Appeal To You, Dear Reader _____ *71*

Resources _____ *75*

References _____ *87*

Notes _____ *91*

FOREWORD

I have always been fascinated with the lifecycle of the butterfly. It is an incredible observation to watch the journey of a butterfly egg from its pupa stage (caterpillar) into the emergence of adulthood, and then a beautifully colored body with wings. It is an amazing transformation to watch this creature as it flies throughout the earth performing its purpose to seek a mate, and create more colorful, breathtaking butterflies before its lifecycle ends.

Similarly, we humans, like the butterfly, journey through life seeking fulfillment of our purpose. However, have we intentionally considered whether we have left a heritage and legacy for our loved ones? Have we implanted a mark or footprint along our life path, or adequately prepared or planned for our demise?

We take many steps toward our goals as we experience varying levels of success and experiences throughout the stages of our lives. During these stages, we do much preparation, planning, coordination and implementing. Subsequently, many appointments are made along the journey. We break many appointments, some we reschedule, and others we commit to keep.

But one appointment many never fully consider or even want to contemplate is that final appointment with death. This is an appointment that not one of us will fail to keep. It is inescapable, and we can be assured that it will happen.

Within these pages I share with you real-life, thought-provoking experiences to help you see in your mind's eye that death inevitably takes us all.

Can you unequivocally say that you have planned for your appointment with death? Do you believe you will take your achievements or assets with you after your demise? After reading through this small guidebook, I suggest you consider doing some self-reflection on these questions. No matter where we are in life or what our age is, no matter how esteemed we think we are in the workplace, in the church, in the community, politically, or as managers of billions of dollars or CEO's of companies…one should be mindful to contemplate—are my earthly affairs in order and … who is the keeper of my soul?

"And the Lord God formed man of the dust of the ground and breathed into his nostrils the breath of life; and man became a living soul." – Genesis 2:7

INTRODUCTION

For generations, mankind with its many cultures, ethnicities, traditions and values, has asked and scientifically researched the questions, *What is death? How does one experience death? Why does man have to die? Can man live forever?* These questions and more surround this great mystery for human beings.

However, I have come to realize in my own short time here on earth that man, with all his vast knowledge, skills, and earthly wisdom, is limited and will always experience times of failure or defeat. The world we live in, as well as the vastness of the universe, is infinite with complexities and knowledge we have not even begun to fathom. Therefore, seeking a greater hope and source beyond our human capabilities seems to me to be the best pursuit in obtaining a better understanding of death. Man must acknowledge that there is a wise, great, authoritative God who is able to perform exceedingly beyond what our finite minds could ever think or ask.

As humans, our thinking is often fixated on various life issues, not always considering that our existence on earth is limited. God has not allowed us to have complete insight into all of the mysteries surrounding death and life. Therefore, I believe we must come to terms with our limitations and recognize that there is one greater than ourselves who is the Creator and Master of life as we know it. I have chosen to accept and believe the one and true eternal God, our Father, who created a Savior which is the Lord Jesus Christ. The Savior helps to cleanse us and turn us from evil, wicked, and dark ways. The Savior helps us recognize that we need reconciliation for the sins and iniquity of our souls. The Savior helps us to see that we live in a world where we must be in relational exchanges with our family members, friends, neighbors, doctors, lawyers, store clerks, police officers, the sick and homeless, the mentally challenged, and the list goes on and on. So, just as God created humans to be in relationships with one another, so it is that there is an expectation that we should establish a constant relationship with our Father God, Savior, and Holy Spirit, who all are One.

Often spoken clichés and truisms say, "Our time on earth is short, our days are numbered, and life is but a vapor," and indeed we find these statements are true as we see that every living, breathing human dies, whether as an infant, a child, a teenager, or an adult. All human life will come to an end. As the scripture and the saying goes, "Ashes to ashes and dust to dust."

However, I ask that each person consider this question: While you are expecting the unavoidable death of your mortal bodies, what are you doing with your life and in your relationships to leave behind a strong heritage, legacy, passing of values, and estate acquisitions for those you love and cherish? In some communities, it is often believed and accepted that there needs to be no preparation or planning for our demise. I disagree.

Contrary to these beliefs in various communities about death and dying, one needs to be knowledgeable and prepared when the spirit of death comes to visit. If we can plan a wedding, a baby shower, a birthday party, an anniversary or graduation celebration, then it stands to reason we should plan and be prepared when death comes for our loved ones, our friends, or even ourselves.

As you read through this book, you will find that I have shared some key stories from personal experiences with the deaths of family, friends, and others whom I have had the pleasure of knowing or being in relationships with. The experiences are meaningful to me and used as examples to show how we go through life sharing, building, bonding, and many times preparing for what we perceive as important events. And yes, these events are important. However, when it comes to transitioning out of this life of flesh on earth, we rarely address the process of "getting our house in order" to meet our Maker.

Just as an airplane is boarded by passengers with the intent of ascending skyward in flight, so it is that our spirit-man will enter another space and time ordered by God. Our soul will indeed take a type of flight upon death, and it is my hope that the stories shared in this book will allow you to begin to reflect more on the death and dying process. Death is a necessary, unavoidable transformation of our earthly vessel.

INTRODUCTION

The Bible declares, "And as it is appointed unto men once to die, but after this the judgment."– *Hebrews 9:27.*

Life will end. Death will come. Are you in a state of readiness?

1

PROCESSING THE UNIMAGINABLE

Whew! Jonathan was so excited about the approaching opportunity to retire at an age earlier than 60! He and his wife Karen had been relatively successful with raising their three children, although they found themselves having to uproot the family on numerous occasions to different states during the course of his various career moves. However, they managed to tackle each new location with the selling of their previous home and the subsequent purchase of a new one without major difficulties. Now, there was still some family drama Jonathan had to deal with regarding his two siblings and three close cousins, who were all raised in the same house with him, during the course of building his career and maintaining things for his wife and family. But now, with his impending retirement, he figured time would be allotted for him to visit and interact more with family members and assist where he could, especially with his Mom aging and facing more medical challenges. Besides, he thought, most of them were either in between being pissed off at him for being successful, or angry at him for not helping out with their mom since their dad had passed 13 years ago. Yet they held to a mindset that they

CHAPTER 1

could always obtain some type of loan or handout from him to help pull them out of some financial distress of their own doing. And while Jonathan would manage to come through in addressing his family members' financial hardships, none of them realized or were concerned about the severe struggles he himself had been battling with his own family, which included his wife's rare kidney disease, and most recently, his adult daughter's injury from a near fatal motorcycle accident.

Nevertheless, after chiding them the other day, he conceded to purchase plane tickets for his one brother and two cousins for an upcoming ski trip while his other brother and cousin decided to stay close to home, along with their spouses, to keep an attentive watch on their Mom.

For many years, Jonathan and Karen had been strategically planning how they were going to move closer to his siblings, cousins, and his mom upon his retirement, so that they could be closer and more available to help with mom's day-to-day care, doctor's appointments, and other encroaching needs. In addition, this move would help his wife have an easier flow of life while continuing to manage her rare illness, and also to help nurse back their adult daughter, who was convalescing at a facility some distance from her parents. Jonathan felt like his daughter needed to be away from her friends who often heavily influenced her to participate in activities that sometimes resulted in severe accidents or messy consequences.

While at his office one day, Jonathan was explaining to his recently appointed protégé about some data on his government contracts and other external accounts. He had just briefed the regional administrator about his training plans for the young apprentice and had signed and sent in his final papers to HR for processing the upcoming retirement move. He was delighted to train this young man with his fresh new ideas for maintaining the accounts that he had worked so diligently to secure and renew down through the years. Besides, it beat having to turn the accounts over to his colleague, Don, who was really the next in line to get the company's larger accounts that Jonathan handled. But Don's misguided values always included a focus on trying to mix business with pleasure, i.e., always trying to see if he could score and eventually date the women involved in negotiating the contract. This offended Jonathan to his Christian core. In addition, Jonathan resented the fact that their regional manager did not want to deal with the issue of Don's inappropriate business behavior, since he was a relative to him by marriage.

Suddenly, during the training session, a knock came on the door of the meeting room where he and his protégé were working. Immediately, Jonathan's manager, Raymond, and the division's special assistant, Candice, hurriedly came in and asked Jonathan to please step out in the hallway for a minute. Oh no! Jonathan thought, *They are going to change their minds and give the accounts to Don anyway!*

Upon exiting the room into the hallway, Jonathan immediately saw his wife Karen standing there with tears pouring out of her eyes uncontrollably. She ran over to his arms. "Jonathan, Baby," she said. "There has been a tragic accident. A plane

CHAPTER 1

crash on the east coast, headed to Buffalo, New York. The ski lodge where Michael and Jessica, and Alice, and Christine were headed. Oh Jon, they are saying that there were no survivors!"

Jonathan's manager and many others watched the TV that was in the lobby in silent horror, while onlookers stopped, listened and watched the terrifying news broadcast and simultaneously watched Jonathan and his wife's reactions.

Jonathan stood frozen like a zombie, not feeling, not hearing anybody or anything, then began to faintly hear the news commentators calling out the names of those individuals listed on the flight itinerary. He heard his brother and cousins' names. He lost feeling in his legs and found himself in the middle of the floor. People were screaming his name, "Jonathan, Jonathan! It's going to be alright … come on, Jonathan, hold on … wake up, wake up."

As he came out of his fainting spell he searched for the loving face of his wife; he turned his head slightly and saw her there amongst a crowd of unfamiliar faces hovering over him. He reached out and grabbed her as they lay on the floor together, sobbing and calling on the name of the Lord Jesus.

Thoughts and questions began to immediately cloud Jonathan's mind. *How do I handle this, God? Do I need to identify their remains? How do I tell Mom? Does she already know? How did she take this unimaginable, horrific news? How do I get their physical remains back to Oregon? How are their children handling all of this? Oh God, who do I call for help to handle this massive crisis for our family? I am the oldest, so I have to figure this all out, right? Is Pastor Giles still available to speak with me about this? I had heard from my brother that he had been gravely ill a while back. Oh God, my brother is dead now! Who is going to help me with all of this? Oh Lord, I need help. Where do I begin? Help, help, help!* Jonathan passes out again.

2

MY HERO TAKES FLIGHT

What a beautiful spring day it was on the campus of Morgan State University in Baltimore, Maryland! Morgan's campus was fervently buzzing with the sounds of students ready for an upcoming spring break. You could hear the lively sounds of the Morgan Bears Marching Machine Band in their practice session. The band was jamming with some mean Earth, Wind & Fire tunes, and pockets of dancing students and staff were sprinkled across the campus. They were sounding so-o-o-o smooth! The McKeldin Center bridge was lit up with students hanging out in various crowds, laughing, joking, and enjoying the beauty of the day and the season. Boyfriends and girlfriends were all hugged up on each other, and everyone was just flowing with smooth vibes, smiles, hugs, and high-fives while grooving to the music of the Bears Band nearby.

There were members of the Morgan Bears Basketball team hanging out on the bridge, too. They were exciting everybody with some of their headline-making moves and jokes, while loudly encouraging everybody to show up at the game on Saturday to support them against North Carolina A&T.

CHAPTER 2

In addition, a group of my friends and I had just left the Science Hall and Holmes Hall after receiving early news from our Physical Science and English professors that our midterm grades were posted. I was elated to find out that I had achieved a B in Physical Science and an A in English. *YAY for me!* I just knew my parents were going to be so proud of me for keeping my grades up during my second year of college.

My Daddy always gave me words of acknowledgement and praise when I did well in my classes. He also sometimes made a way to give me a small gift or special treat for doing well, even though he really could not afford it. My daddy just seemed to marvel at the achievements of his children. He and Momma had six of us, and Dad, although a strict disciplinarian, was an exceptional and loving provider to his children (or the "Deep Six," as he affectionately called us).

He was secretly happy that his firstborn son, my brother Mike, was accepted into the United States military. Even though it was the era of the Vietnam War when he enlisted, and Mike and I feared that they would ship him out at any time for the war, our father still had a sense of pride that his son was serving the country. I believe this was largely because our Dad was rejected several times when he applied to go into military service during his younger years. Therefore, I guess indirectly in some sense, he lived his dream through the experiences of his firstborn son.

We had known Dad as a great and knowledgeable provider. He was always a hardworking man who consistently provided for his wife and six children. He was an exceptional model of manhood and fatherhood for his four sons and two daughters. He taught us all to diligently pursue education and knowledge. He also taught all my brothers how to work and produce with their hands so that they could repair and fix things when it came to obtaining their future homes, for themselves and their families. He also spoke with me at times about my desire to travel and encouraged me to start traveling out of state early in my young adulthood. He always said, "The world is your classroom, daughter." My dad was truly a hero to us all, as he wisely taught us so many practical things about living the best life had to offer.

Dad always desired to travel, and finally had the opportunity to do so in his late 30s and early 40s. He was so excited when he and Mom were able to purchase airline tickets to go visit his brother in San Francisco, California. My dad loved the thrill of a flight taking off. Whether he was on the actual aircraft or just observing the plane taking off on the runway, he was just ecstatic about flights taking off. In fact, his last place of employment was at Friendship International Airport (currently known as the Baltimore-Washington International Thurgood Marshall Airport). I had never seen my daddy so happy as when he landed a job at Friendship Airport. He was able to purchase a new yellow Cadillac after securing employment there. On his days off, he often gathered his children together for a day trip out to the airport so he could show us and describe for us how those big Boeing aircraft could go so high into the sky after taking off from the runway.

CHAPTER 2

It was so meaningful for him to watch these planes take flight and to share the experience with his children.

Back on campus, the spirit of partying, good times, and looking forward to the weekend had us jumping and shaking while we were all out on McKeldin Bridge on that sunny spring day. I saw my friend, DJ (Diana), and we yelled out to each other and ran to catch up on plans for the weekend since classes were done for the day. DJ and I were leaning on the rail of the bridge playing and joking with some of the football guys who were begging us to take the writing proficiency exam for them. They kept saying they would be let go from the team if they did not pass the mandatory University writing proficiency exam. They kept pleading and asking us how much would we charge them to take that exam for them. One of the linebackers for the Bears defense started pulling out $20 and $50 bills, flashing them in my face. I kept dismissing him, but he was persistent in his pleading.

Suddenly their whining and requests faded from my hearing as my eyes glazed over and looked towards the end of the entrance leading up to McKeldin Bridge. I kept staring at a long yellow vehicle that looked like my Daddy's new Cadillac. I kept my focus on the car as the linebacker's pleading became just a distant distraction, while my gaze and attention stayed intently on that yellow Cadillac approaching. Then I yelled out, "DJ, look! It's my Daddy coming up the driveway in his new Cadillac. That's his car!" I couldn't wait to hug and kiss Daddy in his sharp, brand-new Cadillac. But I wondered what he was doing on campus. DJ said, "Girl, are you sure that's him?" I replied, "Yeah," with a puzzled and perplexed feeling, wondering why my daddy would come up to Morgan's campus for me. How did he even know where or how to find me?

I walked briskly with DJ and a few other friends toward the end of the bridge to meet the yellow Cadillac approaching so that I could be sure it was really my father. As we came to the end of McKeldin Bridge and the car slowed down, I squinted my eyes and concentrated intensely on trying to identify the driver of the car. I soon realized it was not my father. As the car slowed and came to a stop, the figure that emerged from my daddy's Cadillac was that of my oldest brother, Mike. He had just recently been discharged from the Army and had only been home for about one week. Mike jumped out of the car when he saw DJ and me. We were still full of excitement and pumped up about the beautiful spring day, as I asked Mike "Why are you up here at Morgan in Daddy's car?" My brother came closer to me with red, teary eyes full of pain, took me by the shoulders with both hands and said, "Dorene, I came looking for you to tell you some terrible news. Daddy has died."

Suddenly, the world began to crash and fall all around me. I couldn't breathe. I couldn't talk. My head was spinning and spinning until all I remembered was going down to the ground. I must have fainted. I could scarcely hear DJ and my other friends saying, "What's wrong? Is Dorene sick? Do we need to take her to the health suite? What is happening? Someone, call the nurse!"

CHAPTER 2

Everything became a blur to me, as my brother said, "I have her, I am taking her to the car." Mike proceeded to practically lift me to the car, with other friends helping him to place me in the seat. DJ and the others gathered up my belongings, which had apparently fallen from my arms to the ground. I couldn't speak. Tears rolled down my face. I kept thinking, *This is not real. This is not happening to me. This is not happening to our family.* I could hear Mike's voice in a distant sort of way, but nothing he said registered. Nothing seemed clear to my mind. I felt numb. I felt lost. I felt angry. I felt hurt with a deep pain I had never experienced before. I was in and out of denial. *Not my Father, he can't be dead ... not breathing anymore, not alive or walking around anymore, not at home for me to hug and talk to. Not my Daddy. This is a dream. He is still alive. He's my father. He's the head of our family. He can't die. Not now.* I didn't understand then how my world was changing at that very second. I did not know how to cope with it at the young age of 19. Why God? *Why did you take my Daddy? Then I remembered my mother. Where is Momma? Is Momma okay?*

Suddenly I snapped out of my delusional, crippling thoughts, and I asked Mike loudly and harshly, "Where is Momma? Take me to Momma." Mike calmly said, "We are going to her right now, Dorene, just take it easy." As we drove along, my thoughts raced back to how I woke up early many mornings as a youngster to the smell of Daddy's fresh coffee brewing, fixed before departing for his workday. I would sit quietly and sleepily on the stair steps just to see my father walk out of the door to begin his workday. Then he would turn around quickly before leaving and say with a big smile on his face, "I see you sitting there, Dean. Come on down." I would slowly move down the stairs to get a hug and kiss from him while he firmly stated, "Be sure to help your mother today." That moment was the last I would have with my daddy. And looking back, I realized that my daddy had taken his final flight without me able to kiss him or say goodbye.

As I reflect on my Daddy's short life on this earth, I recognize that life does indeed go by quickly, like a vapor. We are soon cut off and our soul takes flight.

3

THE DESIGNER'S MASTERPIECE

It was a bustling, beautiful spring in 1997. The weather was getting so warm one would've thought it was surely summertime already. I really did not think this day would finally arrive. I was preparing to receive my graduate degree from Lincoln University, while simultaneously raising my three children, serving as a minister in the church, working full-time as Immunization Bureau Assistant Director, and dealing with a difficult, challenging marriage. My sister-girl, Brenda, pushed me hard, encouraged me every day, and helped me with caring for my kids-all to get us to this moment which we thought I was so far from achieving. Well, here we were, and my sweet momma and favorite Aunt Bert (my usual star champions and dominant family figures). These women were the all-giving nurturers and guidance counselors in life for me, who helped to propel me to this hard-to-believe accomplishment.

Bert came down a few weeks before the actual graduation ceremony and took Momma, Pam, Zakiyya, and me shopping for authentic African attire for the rite of passage ceremony that was an integral part of receiving the Master of Health

CHAPTER 3

& Human Services Degree program for Lincoln's graduate school. Momma was so excited with all the festivities. She and Aunt Liz had even prepared a celebration party event for me down at the Basilica Place Community Room, where Aunt Liz resided. There was so much happening, and Momma had worked hard to make sure I was celebrated and that this occasion would be an event for me to remember for the rest of my life.

Momma had the sweetest and most loving personality. Like her mother, Allean (my grandmother), she always seemed to find good in everybody and generated kindness toward every person that God allowed her life to touch. She always loved her children unconditionally and cared for the physical, emotional, and spiritual needs of her six children. And she demonstrated the same caring, loving ways for all her lineage and church family, in addition to also showering it on her close friends.

Our family delighted in celebrating just about anything. Momma always looked forward to hitting the road with many of us to travel and celebrate good times, good vibes and acknowledging life's accomplishments with her children, family, and friends.

Momma was beaming so much when we first purchased a new home in Woodlawn. We celebrated and partied with many family members, friends, and church family. So many came over and stopped by to help warm the house and make exciting memories that we could cherish forever.

Another wonderful occasion for Momma was when we traveled for Khadija and Francis's fantastic wedding. Although Mom had started to use a wheelchair from time to time, Khadija made sure we had a luxury suite at the hotel in Philadelphia for the wedding event that catered to the needs of her disabled Aunt Vivian. Oh, what a ball we had at the Christmastime wedding of the James-Keating family. I had the sweet task and pleasure of being the minister to officiate and facilitate their wedding vow exchange. Afterward, the delightful wedding festivities began. Momma was clearly so taken and mesmerized at the way Francis and Khadija wowed the reception crowd with their fine, in-step dance moves at the reception. Everyone still talks about those classy moves to this day!

Another phenomenal time of celebration was when many family members traveled to Washington, D.C. for my sister Pam's graduation from Strayer University. Although Momma was using the wheelchair much more during this time, it did not stop her from screaming with joy and exhilaration when Pam walked across that stage to receive her degree from Strayer! I believe Momma and Leon (my brother-in-law), displayed equal excitement about Pam's achievement, to the point that one would have thought that Leon and Momma were receiving that degree as their own! Leon was busily pushing Momma all around that Verizon Center auditorium as we attempted to find Pam immediately after the graduates dispersed from the stage. We were a family of excited people as we marched along in that crowded auditorium, trying to

CHAPTER 3

find each other and locate strategic places to take pictures of all of us with Pam and her degree.

The time came when we had to figure out where we were going to find a restaurant to accommodate our large family to continue celebrating Pam's graduation festivities. Finally, Windell's girlfriend found and reserved a beautiful restaurant for us all at Washington Harbor. We went there and feasted and celebrated, taking more pictures and creating fond memories.

Our Momma did not let being in a wheelchair stop her from participating anyplace we celebrated family milestones and events. There were so many great festivities that she insisted on being a part of and nothing stopped us from providing whatever transportation she needed to get her to some of the out-of-state destinations that our family and friends were part of.

We had more celebrations in Harrisburg, PA when we went to Sharia and Bill's new house up on the hill in the mountainous section of Harrisburg. In addition, we were always travelling to be a part of the plays and events that Sharia produced at Greater Zion Church. Sharia functioned as Greater Zion's Youth and Family Life Pastor. Her plays were so breathtaking and extraordinary, Momma always had to be there to see it all unfold on stage.

Another occasion for Mom to travel was when Peewee informed us that Zhondria had been accepted at Georgetown University and was presented with a plethora of basketball scholarships. Peewee shared that Zhondria had decided to play for Georgetown and became an official Georgetown Hoya!

Momma was always overjoyed and involved with all the great successes of her grandchildren. She helped organize Zakiyya's (my daughter) 16th birthday party at the Cheesecake Factory. When Zakiyya went to college, Momma was determined to see the dormitory at the college in Takoma Park, MD where Zakiyya would be living. Even though Momma's disability impeded her ability to effectively walk, and there were no elevators in this Seventh Day Adventist college, our mother had a fierce determination to go up the steps on her butt to the third-floor dormitory room where her granddaughter would live throughout the semester. She went up step by step until she reached the top floor.

Momma always exhibited her steadfastness of faith to prove she could accomplish many things despite her disability. She always delighted in hearing her granddaughter, Raizel, play the piano keyboard and sing. Momma always believed that Raizel would be anointed to sing before the Lord as her gift.

When Little Kevin married Mandy and moved to Australia, Momma looked like her heart would break. However, she always prayed hard for them and looked forward to the telephone calls they would make to her, which always increased the joy in her day or week. She was delighted to be at the graduation and prom for her grandson, Joshua. She was an avid attendee at Joshua's musical events when he sang in the

CHAPTER 3

Maryland State Boys Choir and she was especially excited to attend the speeches that her grandson, Jamal, gave as a member of 100 Strong Young Men Club in his high school. Momma was thrilled when Jamal graduated from high school and decided he would go to a community college, since he always declared he was tired of going to school and would not attend college.

Her grandchildren were her extra set of children that she adored and constantly spoiled. She often provided babysitting services for her grandchildren, Tiffany, Zhondria, Raizel, Zakiyya, Joshua, Jamal, Dante, Aaron, Windell, Mooco and little Kevin. She also frequently picked her grandchildren up from school and provided good hot meals for them until their parents retrieved them later in the evening after work. To further nurture and guide her grandchildren as they developed into adulthood, she graciously allowed some of them to live in her home so she could support them in their endeavors to transition into healthy adults. Her grandson Dante lived with her for several years and faithfully attended church services and activities with her. And her granddaughter Zakiyya was blessed to live in her home for a couple of years as well.

Although Mom's health began to decline and become more challenging to handle, her "Deep Six" children remained faithful in helping her to manage and cope at every turn. The six of us began to have regular family meetings to discuss our next course of action to help Mom have the best quality of life as her disability began to take its toll on her body. Nothing kept her from going to church and being in the house of the Lord. She went by wheelchair and had four strong sons to make sure her delivery to and from church was always a smooth success. Anywhere Mom was to be lifted or carried, her four sons were at the ready and on standby to perform the needed task to make sure she never had to ask for assistance from anyone else for transportation needs.

Our mom always kept a clean, classy, orderly home, and she loved to entertain and have friends and family over. As her three oldest, Mike, Pam, and I began to notice the difficulty she started to have with regard to cleaning her house. We also noticed clear signs of struggle with her own self-care. Because she was a private and independent woman in all respects, it was hard for us to convince her that she needed an assistant in the house to help care and watch for her while we all worked during the day at our respective places of employment. She finally conceded once we located a girlfriend and fellow churchgoer, Annie Harris, to help her with daily hygiene and house cleaning efforts. It made Momma's day to know that someone she—and we—trusted would be assisting her with daily chores and self-care responsibilities.

It was at this point in her life that Momma pushed and prodded me and Pam to help get her house in order. She wanted me to prepare her power of attorney papers, her will, and find out about signing a healthcare directive. She insisted that Pam stay on task with paying all her bills on time. She was so very conscious and adamant about me completing these legal documents that when I would say, "Mom, I'm too tired tonight, I will get around to doing it," she kept telling

CHAPTER 3

me not to say that and for me to make the time to complete these documents for her. Being an obedient daughter, I did as she requested.

Harder times came for us in caring for Momma, as she did have some falls and diabetes issues that caused her body and skin to break down in some areas. As her children, we were tasked with making difficult medical choices and decisions in concert with her doctors and in addition, we always consulted with our Aunt Bert, who lived in Illinois. My oldest brother, Mike, decided to move back into the house with Momma so he could be there after he got off work to help address anything associated with Momma's healthcare needs. Her oldest grandson, Moo-co, also made it part of his commitment and routine to come to her house and help care for some of her daytime needs as well. Because Peewee, Pam and I made sure she got to all appointments to see her wound care doctors and specialists, it eventually became necessary for Pam and myself to alternate every other evening to clean and change the dressings on her flesh wounds. This was a task that she only wanted her two daughters to handle, since the wounds were in a very private area.

I researched and consulted with attorneys, family, and friends until I obtained the required information to get Mom's will, POA, and health care directive documents exactly how she wanted them. I am so grateful that I obeyed her and stayed on task with completing all of the necessary documents while her mind was still sharp, and she was able to speak her desires. Getting names of people and items listed on paper exactly

THE DESIGNER'S MASTERPIECE

how she wanted things to be after her demise, was a successful and needful activity, that I was happy to complete.

Mom's 77th birthday was approaching, and the spirit of the Lord nudged me to do a big festive celebration in recognition of the upcoming event. I shared it with some of our older family members and some of her longtime friends. While many folks suggested that I wait until the more traditional 80th birthday to do a big celebration, I kept insisting that we needed to do a big grand celebration for Momma on her 77th birthday, which fell on August 3, 2012. So, after enlisting my sister's help, we started planning for Mom's big party around March 2012. We searched for venues and developed the invitation list, busying ourselves with all the detailed preparations. We also had fun keeping the big surprise a secret, so Mom didn't figure out what we were up to. To keep her from being so inquisitive, we told her we were planning to take her to a special hotel for a birthday getaway and fancy dinner. Of course, the birthday celebration was a smashing success and she was super surprised! While we did book her in a hotel room for the weekend, she had no idea that over 100 guests—family and friends—were waiting at the hotel conference center and restaurant for her to arrive so they could greet her with a big shout-out surprise. What a phenomenal occasion it was! Mom was astonished, excited, and so grateful to see so many people there to help celebrate her 77 years of life. Later, after all the festivities ended, Mom, Pam and I went to the hotel room to finish opening all her gifts and cards. She was like a 10-year-old girl, animated, thrilled and ecstatic

CHAPTER 3

that we had done all of this for her. As tired and sleepy as my sister and I were, Mom could not stop talking and reliving the evening. She kept me and Pam up all night retelling the wonderful experiences of everything that was done and said at her birthday party celebration. What sensational Jesus joy to see our Mom so extremely happy, even during her great periods of pain and suffering.

As we entered the season and time when Momma had to be increasingly in and out of hospital care, or in and out of nursing home rehab care, she was challenged with bouts of dementia. In addition, long periods of severe episodic pain became commonplace for our dear Momma, causing her to scream and cry out at any given time during the day or night.

We had been meeting and communicating with her doctors more and more concerning Mom's medical conditions. As she declined to eat less and less and talked about seeing her deceased Mom and Dad and her deceased sisters, we began to realize that we had to start preparing for her transition. I soon recognized how earthly things no longer mattered to Mom anymore. Her dementia episodes took her in and out of talking with deceased family members and little to no conversations to those of us that were living. She kept asking us to help take away her pain. Dementia started becoming more frequent, and all of us experienced personal pain, fearing the loss and separation of our dear sweet Queen and dominant guiding family force. This great masterpiece of God was preparing to take her final flight, choosing to live in eternity with the Savior, rather than continue suffering in the pain of her flesh.

She knew the time was coming for her departure. That is why she made the necessary preparations for her transition from earth to God's glory. She wanted all to be well with her soul.

The load was getting heavier for us, but Mom had prepared us for the impending transition she would have to experience. She had appointed me as her primary POA, with Pam as backup POA. The doctors encouraged us to consider a referral to hospice. After speaking with all our siblings and Aunt Bert, it was determined that she would be transported from Good Samaritan Hospital in northeast Baltimore to the Stella Maris Hospice Center in Lutherville, Maryland.

Full of God's wisdom and overflowing with much grace, our Vivian (Mom) had poured into all six of us unconditional love beyond measure, along with deep-seated, strong family values. She knew these items were key and instrumental toward carrying us throughout life to handle any negative or ungodly force that would challenge us. These gems of value were worth more than any amount of gold or silver. In addition, it was essential to pour these lessons of life and wisdom into future generations so they would continue to be deposited into the future lineage of our dear Mother.

A treasure more valuable than gold, a love and joy undefined by mere mortal words. Momma, you were the masterpiece that God created especially for us. It is because you were that we are. Mom's spirit lives on through her devoted, steadfast Deep Six.

4

ANOTHER FATHER TO ME

What fun times we had during our undergraduate years at Morgan State University. School breaks during Thanksgiving, Christmas, and spring were full of fun, travel, hustle, and bustle.

I loved going to spend Thanksgiving or any weekend during the fall and winter with my girl, DJ. We often looked forward to packing our bags to stay a long weekend in her hometown of Westchester County, New York. We knew Ma Jones (DJ's mom) was going to hook us up with some serious food to stuff our freezer with when we traveled back to school in Baltimore.

As everyone hung out on Morgan's McKeldin Bridge talking about holiday food, certain professors, and getting their midterm grades, I nestled back into my own private daydream about riding the train to upstate New York. I was looking forward to getting away since my Momma had started dating this "Mr. Brown" guy, of whom I was not very fond.

After midterms were over, DJ and I always had a small get-together at our apartment with a few of our college buddies. Since it was holiday time, we asked a few extra friends and

CHAPTER 4

neighbors to come over. After hanging out with everyone, watching a few movies, and listening to music, we started letting everyone know it was time to go because we had a train to catch in the morning. After all the folks were gone, we went into a whirlwind of cleaning up the apartment. We cleaned our bedrooms, bathrooms, even shook out the floor rugs, all to make sure our place would be fresh and clean once we returned from New York. We had good neighbors who always looked out for our place when we were out of town. We trusted them with a spare set of keys so they could also water our plants and take in the mail. We'd packed our suitcases the night before, so we would not have to do very much before leaving for the train station.

DJ and I always strategically packed for our trips up to the big state of New York. DJ would always give me "the talk" about how we were supposed to handle ourselves when we got to New York City's Grand Central Station. She used to make me kind of nervous with these discussions because she always emphasized how quickly trouble could happen for travelers going in and out of Grand Central. She was especially fond of telling me about the criminals who had polished the art and skill of pickpocketing. These criminals prided themselves with being able to steal money, wallets, ID cards, and personal effects of the many travelers who came through Grand Central. DJ taught me how to place my money, ID cards, and other needed personal items for travel way down deep in my jean pockets, or in a small pouch that I would layer under my clothing, so as to not be visible or easily accessible to suspected thieves or robbers.

The next day, once we finished our final packing, and I called to check in with my Mom, we were ready to call a cab to head out to Penn Station. We did a final check-in with our friends and neighbors, then headed out the door.

By the time we arrived at the humongous Grand Central in NYC, it was about 6:30 p.m. That place was so alive and loud, with thousands of people walking super-fast in every direction taking my breath away. People constantly bumped into each other without caring whether anyone apologized for the abrupt collision. DJ and I explored Grand Central while waiting for our train. It seemed the trains west were always late with the added inconvenience of long layovers. I guess that was partly because of the holiday season. I was so mesmerized by the hustle and bustle of NYC that I always had lots of questions for DJ about the city that never slept. However, during our exploring the huge icon of New York's busiest transportation hub, we managed to pick up some special items for niece Yo-Yo and big sister Jenny. We were also conscious of keeping our eyes and ears alert for the announcement of train departures and gate entry for Westchester County. If we missed our train boarding time, it meant waiting a much longer time for the next train going up to Peekskill in Westchester County.

Once we boarded our train, it was much later in the evening. We found some good comfortable seats, pulled out our blankets and prepared to nestle in for a long nap while heading up North via the Hudson Line.

CHAPTER 4

When we got off the train at the Peekskill stop, we immediately looked for DJ's father (Pa Jones), as he was always faithful to pick us up at the train depot. Pa Jones was a wonderful, smart, extremely kind and endearing man. He was always so excited to see DJ and me. He had such a good heart and beautiful smile. He was always about the business of making others feel special. On the ride home from the train station, Pa Jones elaborated on how Ma Jones (DJ's mother), had fixed all our favorite things to eat. In addition, he made mention of all the family members around town that we had to get up early to go visit the next morning.

Once we arrived at Ma and Pa Jones's house in Peekskill, DJ and I walked through the door to the wondrous, familiar smells of Ma Jones's cooking. Oh my, how this woman could cook, bake and set a table full of phenomenally good foods! Ma Jones literally had the table fully spread with all kinds of meats, vegetables and desserts. Even though our arrival time was usually late at night when we arrived in Peekskill, it didn't matter to Ma Jones. She always prepared a massive spread of delicacies for us as if she were feeding ten people. When we arrived, she immediately grabbed DJ and me and kissed our faces. Next, she was talking about how skinny we were and how we were not eating enough. She went into fussing mode about how we needed to eat better and not stay up all night studying or hanging out with our friends at school. Then we heard the rapid sound of little feet racing down the stairs as DJ's little niece, Yo-Yo, appeared screaming and jumping into her Auntie DJ's arms. Right behind Yo-Yo was her mom,

Jennie, grinning and laughing while slapping and hugging DJ and me on the shoulders.

After all the hugs and kisses were done, DJ and I settled in to eat and talk with the womenfolk. Pa Jones disappeared into the living room area to relax and partake of his pipe. The tobacco had a sweet-smelling, cherry aroma, a scent that was so distinguishable to him. I adored its smell because it always reminded me of him. This reserved man of courage and quiet strength was considerate and loving to his family. When he accepted me as one of his own daughters, my heart was overjoyed. I lost my daddy to diabetes and heart condition, and Mr. Charles Jones, Sr. genuinely accepted me as another member of the Jones family.

He never ceased to show me good times with the rest of the family. The next morning after sleeping for a few hours, DJ and I had to get up and get ready to be driven around the small town to Aunt Tot's, Cousin Cookie's, and all the rest of the other family members' homes. At every house we were expected to eat and drink something fancy.

However, before leaving the house that morning, we had a charming and friendly visit from Bones, DJ's older brother. Unlike DJ, Bones was always reserved and humble. However, we did find out he really had a passion for golf, though you wouldn't know it by his unassuming manner. Nevertheless, he always made sure he headed over to his parents' home when his little sister was visiting from college.

CHAPTER 4

During one of my visits to upstate NY, Pa Jones took me to visit the West Point Naval Academy. Oh, what a great honor and pleasure it was to see this famous place and to watch the young military cadets move with precision and discipline, dressed in full military uniform. During another visit, Pa Jones took us all out to the base of a great mountain where we had a wintertime picnic with huge thermos bottles of hot chocolate, and everyone jumped onto the big rink to go ice-skating. That great place was known as Bear Mountain, located in Orange County New York, in the Hudson Highlands. It has become one of my favorite places in the world to visit. Some of my fondest memories were created with Ma and Pa Jones, DJ, Yo-Yo, Bones, and Jennie, as well as Aunt Tot, Aunt Elsie, Uncle Hop, and so many others in Peekskill and White Plains, New York.

So, when I received the news from my buddy DJ that Pa Jones had passed, my heart sank very deeply into a depressive state. The myeloma cancer had taken its toll on his body. I was devastated for Ma Jones, DJ, Bones and the whole family. Pa's presence was a mainstay; I did not think he would be taken from us so soon. He was a real father figure to me, and a giant of a man to his whole family. I can still smell the sweet odor of his tobacco as he retreated to the living room to take his chair and light his pipe. The smell of his tobacco will always take me back to a place and time of joy, security, and homely comforts. Whenever he and Ma Jones visited DJ and I at our apartment in Baltimore during our college days, they faithfully took us to the grocery store to make sure our freezer and refrigerator was over full. Their visits were so regular and so very normal that I always expected to see them again and again. However, I have come to greatly understand the seasons we all go through in life and that each life, no matter how precious to us, must come to an end. Even the best of those we love seem to die younger or sooner than we expect. It just seems it is always just too soon!

And so, we face this encounter with the death of a loved one and move on in our mourning until we reach a place of healing from our sorrows. Pa Jones left a phenomenal legacy—to be accountable, kind, caring, and to always consider others. He was quite the definition of manhood; so many of us are eternally grateful for the footprints he left during his journey on earth. Thankfully, preparations were made for this Korean war hero's demise, whose memory lives on eternally in our hearts.

5

CHURCH AND FAMILY ICON

The regal, statuesque, God-fearing, ministering woman arose and opened her eyes. It was another blessed day of life that God saw fit for her to see. She began chuckling to herself as she looked up to the heavens and asked her usual question to her Maker. "Lord, why am I still here?"

Beginning the day as usual, she started her morning prayer before the Lord and repented for questioning Him about her time here on earth. Then the usual ritual began of meticulously putting on each article of clothing, combing her hair, and finally putting on her finery, pearls and a sweater pin. She was an impeccable dresser and fashionable lady. She loved hats and finer accessories, and always dressed as a true and noble lady. After completing her outfit and stroking that last comb or brush through her hair, she subsequently looked into the mirror with a nod and said, "Not too bad, ol' girl. You looking good for this seasoned age of 95+ years."

With a final tug to pull up her hosiery, she glanced down to slide into a pair of her Sunday best shoes. She then pulled the wheelchair to her bedside and transferred her worn, frail body from the bedside to the chair. Off she went down the halls

CHAPTER 5

of the facility to greet all her friends and the medical staff. It was time for her to talk about the goodness of the Lord to those she encountered during her wheelchair stroll through the hallways.

As her facility friends came slowly out of their rooms, they began to gather around her to celebrate her beauty and how well she looked. They made excited remarks of "Ooh," and "Aaah," about how well-dressed she was, the beautiful curls in her hair, and the jewelry she adorned herself with.

As the wife of a Bishop, she was a faithful companion to her husband. As they built their lives together, they helped to grow the church and support the people of God in a dedicated and loving manner. She worked tirelessly in the church while functioning as church clerk/secretary, developing and organizing choirs for the church, establishing auxiliaries like the Church Missionary Board. She was a knowledgeable and premier Sunday school teacher who taught all levels of classes but held a special devotion to teaching and grooming aspiring young ministers. She also led the Church Education Department as Sunday School Superintendent. She operated as a church trustee board member and was always eager to coordinate various church fundraisers and bus trips to help introduce the church members to different sights and places of travel to God's earthly creations in other states. Going to Luray Caverns, Longwood Gardens, the Pennsylvania Dutch Amish country, and to Niagara Falls, were just a few of the many bus trips she organized to bring family and friends together for educational journeys.

She was a woman of hospitality and had much love for family and good friends that produced great and memorable times. She and her husband were fond of helping people, by opening up their home to assist couples and individuals facing hard times. Over the years they had opened the second floor of their home to many who would live there until a good job came through, or until their financial situation improved. She was a seasoned cook and you could often find many good aromas throughout her home when paying her a visit. The sound of clacking pots and pans was always heard as she threw together a good meal to serve to her family and guests entering in and out of her home down through the years. And her dish of candied sweet potatoes was a long time favorite of those near and far.

To know her was to revere her, adore her, honor her, and love her. In her presence, one was sure to receive wisdom and revelation of God's esteemed Holy word. She was a Regal Woman of God ... an Elect Lady to the body of Christ Jesus.

On the day of her death, it was described that after about 15 minutes into the hallway, she let out a cry of pain. Her friends called and motioned for the medical personnel to come quickly. When asked what happened, she iterated that the pain had come to her side near her stomach. With no known history of stomach problems, the attendant asked her if she would like to go to the bathroom and she agreed to go. She tried to pass her bowel and was successful at doing so. The attendant rolled her back into her room thinking the problem was resolved, however she cried out again, looked up to the

CHAPTER 5

heavens and asked the Lord, "What is this unknown pain I am experiencing, dear Lord?" After a moment she whispered, "Okay Lord, I thank you." It was at that moment, it was reported, that her soul took flight.

Suddenly, the attendant noticed she was having a bit of a struggle breathing, and emergency services were called. By the time help arrived, her soul had transitioned forward to meet with her Maker and Savior.

Regal. Statuesque. This woman was a keeper of finer things like her lead crystal vases and porcelain china place settings. She adored luxury and especially loved driving her Lincoln Continental Town Car for which her husband always made provision for her to have the latest model. She owned a set of hand gloves for many of her outfits, along with a matching hat to complete her look. She was the wife of a bishop and a great minister, and a missionary and teacher of God's word. She was always mindful during the Christmas holiday season to thoughtfully shop, shop, shop for those on her list. Focused and inclined, she found a special gift for just about everyone she knew.

Many young Christian women often visited at home or sat attentively at her knee to receive instruction on femininity, Christian Sisterhood, duties of a wife, and the art of prayer and being a student of the Bible. Though she was without natural children, she had many Godchildren and Spiritual sons and daughters, that she nurtured, loved, and poured gifts into. She was also well known for helping to groom Pastor's

Wives and Missionaries. She was mindful to reach out to her dear neighbors and would make regular telephone calls to her girlfriends for day-time getaways, like shopping, visiting new restaurants, or just taking a drive up 95 North or down 95 South, to look at new places to explore for church activities.

When her days were coming to an end, it was discovered that she had put just as much thought into planning and preparing for her own demise as she also did with everything else in her life. How thoughtful and astute this woman was! She realized early on in life that planning for death was as essential as living life to the fullest. There were three people she had spoken clearly and directly to about how she wanted her funeral to be, the distribution of her belongings, and to whom. These individuals kept records about her directions and decisions. They made sure her wishes were carried out as she had described to them. As she would often say, "I am making sure I have my spiritual and financial house in order for whenever the Lord calls me home to Glory. Therefore, having obtained help from God, I continue until this day."

This amazing woman was full of wisdom, grace, and had a storehouse of Biblical knowledge that could put many to shame. How great was her service to God and toward others. Her legacy, purpose, and footprint has clearly been established on the earth.

6

GANG ALLEGIANCES

It was such a hot, sticky summer day, the kind where beads of sweat rolled profusely down our faces, mixed with tears of sorrow. Ricky was 24 years old, and the church was packed for his funeral. As his body lay stretched out in the casket at the front of the church, there were fierce sobs of tears and screams from his mother, sister, girlfriends, and his baby mamas.

There was such a tense, heavy atmosphere during this funeral, mostly because the sanctuary was filled with members of the gang called the Bloods. Although Ricky had been raised up in church and baptized "in the name of Jesus," he somehow found his way back out into the streets where he proclaimed the Bloods gang as his closest family. Although his parents were ministers in the church and kept him and his siblings involved in youth church activities most of their lives, he had professed his allegiance as a devout member of this Bloods gang. The gang activities he was committed to led to his short lifespan on earth. He was shot and killed amid movements and actions with the rival gang known as the Crips. Ricky's death now packed the church with members of his Bloods

CHAPTER 6

gang, as well as some notable members of the Crips gang in attendance as well.

The atmosphere at church vacillated between somberness to fear to a heightened nervousness. Ricky's parents and family were also spewing out expressions of discord and quarrelsome behavior, due to their disapproval of the strong gang presence in their church and their indifference towards their pastor and church family. This pastor had passionately and faithfully guided Ricky in times past and watched him grow up in the church.

The pastor, who was a devout God-fearing leader, refused to allow the house of the Lord to be disrespected because these gangs chose his church to inappropriately display their gang loyalties with colors, handshakes, and showing off evidence of their concealed weapons. They also verbally boasted of the perceived power of their gang relations in order to intimidate one another and ignite trepidation in the atmosphere of the funeral. The pastor, who had steadily observed all this negative activity, displayed strong restraint as he tried to control his anger at what was going on. Suddenly, he stood up and strode to the microphone, speaking with a strong booming voice which stopped all the disrespectful actions in their tracks and commanded the attention of everyone in that sanctuary.

He acknowledged the bereaved family, the church family, and a few others and then bellowed out fierce words, punctuated with Godly power, authority, and faith. His voice became larger than life, and his stature seemed gigantic compared to any other man in that sanctuary as he declared to all who were present: "I want you all to know that in this sanctuary we have dedicated power to our great and mighty God, and it will not be disrespected! I will not tolerate loud laughter, the commonplace attitude of some of you gang members, who think you are in control in our house—a house of prayer for the Lord. This is my territory, not the domain for your gang or your gang leaders, period. Now know that Jesus Christ is the chief cornerstone over this place, and we fear no man; only God himself is to be feared and revered in this place. Now all of you gang members with your weapons, obey and respect this place while you are in my House. You need to start by bringing all your weapons to the altar of God right now. You can receive them back after we serve this family by having a decent service about the life of this young man and then commit his body to burial. If you cannot obey and adhere to this request, you will leave right now. I fear no man. My Lord and my God will defend me and fight for me."

After two minutes of silence and no movement in the sanctuary, there was a tenseness and then a shift in the atmosphere began. Several young men lined up in the middle aisle and walked up to the altar to lay down their guns. Many followed suit, slowly and calmly. These young men were either dressed in red or dressed in blue, each in their respective gang's colors of allegiance. One member reached out to the pastor to ask if there could be a designated church officer standing by to watch over the respective piles of weapons, along with one member of their gang to stand watch as well. After the pastor

CHAPTER 6

agreed, and all was established, everyone could see and feel the atmosphere shifting to one of respect and calmness.

Ricky had often visited and would come back to the church decorated in his red gang colors (which the Bloods stood by as their color), mainly out of love and respect for his mom and the pastor. The interesting thing with these return visits was that he would stay a while and participate in Sunday school sessions or stay to hear the whole sermon that was being preached by the pastor. Oftentimes, Ricky would also stay to engage the pastor in a one-to-one session, or he would just stay around and sit under the arms of one of the church mothers or stay hugged up with his own momma.

After the pastor preached the funeral, the family ordered that there be one final viewing. Many of the Bloods gang members walked up to the casket and began placing all types of Bloods paraphernalia in the casket next to Ricky's body. There were red scarves, red cigars, red painted wine bottles or liquor bottles, red flags, and pictures framed in red. His female friends or mothers of his babies placed all types of indescribable items that also had red on them. The filled-up casket was quite a sight for the church members. They were not accustomed to this type of behavior for honoring the dead. Additionally, and of note, when the mortician went to close the casket, it was very difficult, considering all the items that had been placed inside. However, they managed to complete the task with so many eyes watching to make sure their articles of memorabilia were included when the casket closed.

The death of this young man (and former gang member) was a painful situation for many to experience. It was even more painful for the family, because there was no insurance policy in place to help with the burial of this young brother whose life was taken on the streets by the gang life he chose to be a part of.

Unfortunately, the family had to seek donations and assistance from the church congregants and other social resources in order to provide a decent burial and bring closure to the young life that many loved and had high hopes for. Surely preparation for death is needed no matter the age of a soul. And no matter how small an inheritance left behind after one's transition from earth, discussion for one's demise should be addressed as early in life as possible. And then occasionally reviewed to update legal documents as life events change over the course of our lives.

During the 1980s and 1990s, East Coast Crips and Bloods gangs were very prominent in Baltimore, Maryland. The Bloods were more heavily infiltrated in Baltimore neighborhoods than the Crips. Their presence was substantial, and they greatly influenced young African American and Latino men. There was also a small percentage of Native American young men involved in their gangs as well. Churches experienced a great loss of young male Christian churchgoers. However, the lure of young men into this fast lane of gang life appeared more enticing and family-like to them than their biological or church families. What lessons are we to learn from this?

7

AN UNEXPECTED DEATH

Delicate, soft layers of white and pink fabric arrayed the casket of this sweet, innocent, 10-year-old. Her angelic face looked as if she were peacefully sleeping and about to wake up and stretch to prepare for another day of school, fun, and ballet dancing with friends. However, her tragic end came sooner than anyone could have imagined. Her loss pierced the heart of just about everyone in attendance, and all could visibly see the indescribable pain for her parents, whose depth of agony could not be understood, except by God alone.

A West Baltimore community and elementary school mourned as if it would never recover from the severe scar that had interrupted its way of life. This included the worry and concern that had risen for the safety of every child in its neighborhood. The senseless attack and murder of this promising young musical star of dance and theatre had crushed the hopes and dreams of so many who knew her and believed in the future of her success.

Teachers, local politicians, school administrators, police officers, community leaders, and so many more influential

CHAPTER 7

individuals attended the funeral to pay their respects to the hurting family and neighborhood. This young princess had so much talent and hope for a bright future in the art of dance and theatre.

Today, innocent children in urban communities are being accidentally shot, injured, and murdered at an alarming rate due to illegal weapons in the hands of unauthorized users. Mindsets have developed that have no regard for human life, whether that life belongs to an infant, a youngster, or a senior citizen. The day and time have come where some people carry out negative or illegal activities with no thought to the consequences of endangering an innocent bystander who happens to be in the path of their evil goal.

Although this beautiful young soul is now gone, her parents had planned early for their family, and all the children had trust funds as well as life insurance, just in case the time ever came that it would be needed. They didn't know or believe the policy would have to be used so soon; it was just an additional precautionary measure they decided to include with their own insurance policies. To them, it was just an act of common sense that had been taught to them by their family's preceding generations. They were instructed to be prepared for the good and the bad in life.

We live in times when evil acts are becoming more prevalent. No one wants to believe that it will happen in their family. However, misfortune can come upon any one of us at any time. Are you prepared in the event of an unexpected death?

8

WHEN A LENGTHY ILLNESS ARRIVES

In this life we live, almost every activity we encounter or go through consists of a process or series of steps that we must adhere to or go through to reach our desired destination or goal. The dying and death experience has its own process too.

While it is appointed unto mankind once to die and then be judged by God Almighty, it is also commanded of each of us to live this life to the fullest. Living to the fullest means to love fervently and with great passion, because on *any* given day, at any second, our lives can be subject to perishing without notice.

Many of us have loved ones whose experience with death will be an elongated process with major illness. While this is an agonizing period for the loved one to go through, as well as for the circle of close family and friends, we must be mindful to make the best of the tense and uncertain atmosphere that the dying process engulfs us in.

Hopefully there will be a designated, strong, dominant family figure that can help lead the family during this traumatic

CHAPTER 8

decision-making time. This is where documents called, "Power of Attorney (POA)", and "Advanced Health Care Directive (AHCD)," are important to have prepared, with up-to-date signatures and final wishes in place. The POA will have been compiled while the loved one was alert, stable, and presented with soundness of mind and consciousness.

Before a sick loved one is considered or documented by medical personnel as not being able to make adequate decisions for themselves, which is usually due to an illness impacting the loved one's ability to reason or make rational choices, a previously prepared POA or AHCD will be the legal document to represent them and convey their wishes. These are the documents that doctors, nurses, and other medical or legal persons will be asking for copies of in addition to a will. In the case of having a POA, a designated person will be listed on the document to speak on behalf of the terminally ill loved one. It is important to understand that if these documents have not been previously completed, notarized, and secured by the family, then this opens up the door for more emotional pain, anguish, stress, and irrational behavior, which may heighten and escalate to an unfavorable scene at the loved one's sick bed.

High level and/or unstable *emotions*, unfortunately, are usually what human beings act on and operate under when the process of dying is occurring for a loved one. This is particularly true if there is no written will, POA, or Advanced Health Care Directive, etc. prepared by the loved one and the family in advance. However, it is important to remember that this is the time where unity, love, peace, understanding, and tranquility should be present for the atmosphere of the loved one. This period is sacred and should be a time and opportunity for family and friends to focus on providing the best quality of life, during whatever time is left, for the loved one's earthly journey. In addition, it is important to remember that the final months, days, and hours, are to be looked upon as precious and tender, as our loved one prepares to make their exit from their earthly existence. The human senses are usually heightened during the dying process and it is key to listen to any final words or requests the loved may be wanting to convey to all who are present.

Also, I must say right here that I honor and greatly respect hospices. These are specially established places that gingerly care for a terminally ill loved one throughout the end stage of life and the dying process. The nurses, doctors, counselors, and support persons that work in the field of death and dying are past being phenomenal people, in my opinion. The gifted persons that are committed to work in hospices are exceptional and full of love, patience, and tenderness. In my experience of watching them work with families, they have displayed more sensitivity, understanding, and gentleness than many of the loved one's close family members or friends. I applaud all that hospice workers do to make a terminally ill loved one's passage peaceful and smooth. They are indeed a rare and precious creation.

While your loved one is in a hospice, do not expect that they will transition in a day or two. On the contrary, hospice

CHAPTER 8

patients have been known to live weeks or even months before dying. In Nurse Barbara Karnes' booklet, *Gone From My Sight*, she describes the various stages or characteristics that family members can expect to look for as the loved one experiences the dying process. She states that one to three months prior to death, they may begin to withdraw and verbally acknowledge that they are dying. Nurse Karnes writes," … this is becoming a time of withdrawing from everything outside of one's self and going inside … where there is sorting out and evaluating of one's self." This is relative to Piaget's theory on the cognitive and intellectual development stages in life, as well as human behavior. He believed humans change in their characteristics as they grow older and that they are adaptive to their end-of-life processing.

Nurse Karnes further suggests that processing of a loved one's life is usually done with their eyes closed, so sleep increases. Although food is a way to energize our bodies, and a means to keep our bodies going, the loved one going through the dying process exhibits a gradual decrease in eating habits. They may verbalize that nothing tastes good anymore. They may prefer liquids over solid foods, and state, "I just do not feel like eating anymore." Nurse Karnes further writes that disorientation may begin to be exhibited one to two weeks prior to death, and our loved one may want to sleep most of the time during this process. Physical changes may be observed, like body temperature fluctuating between fever and cold. Notable breathing changes may be present, along with increased perspiration, and changes in skin color. There is a restlessness that may be noticed, and congestion may be very loud, where the loved one may have to be positioned on one side or the other. In addition, our loved one may become non-responsive or unable to respond in their environment. These things and more are indications that family members should be mindful of.

When a loved one is in hospice, surrounded by expert love and care, you may want to consider using this time to make decisions on final arrangements. It is okay to begin gathering and writing the obituary if it has not already been started or completed. This may also be a good time to begin visiting morticians to decide on whose services you will be using. It is also an opportune time to have conversations with your pastor, minister, and other church family you may want to enlist or engage for help.

Please remember, the most important things in life are not t-h-i-n-g-s! Rather, we should thank God for what we have and be in harmonious relationships with one another. We should not be argumentative or exhibit rage or discontent while at the bedside of a loved one who is in transition. It is the love and kindness that we show toward other human beings that reflects the best treasure. We should be mindful to speak kindly and help others when we can. We do not know if it is the last time we will see a person again. So, let's exhibit tenderness, keep our promises, and do our best to work hard, be happy and share happiness while giving a smile. "Please" and "thank you" are still important key words to say. We should be thankful and grateful for what we have and should trust in the

CHAPTER 8

Lord with all our heart, mind, and soul. Do not allow time (at least not over three days), to pass without extending a heart of forgiveness and generosity toward one another.

For we all have an appointed time at death's door which we must keep, and after that, the judgement.

REFLECTIONS

When the death of a loved one happens in our lives, we are often so emotionally distraught that our rational minds no longer seem to process thoughts in a normal fashion. We can experience many facets of sorrow. Confusion, displacement, and the sense of loneliness are some of the identifiable emotions that begin to take over and may make us feel we are spinning in an uncontrollable sort of way. Physical weakness and unexpected bodily dysfunction may occur, changing our sense of what was previously perceived as normal.

Questions surge forth from our grief-stricken human minds such as, "Why Lord? Why now? Is this really happening to me, to our family?" We begin to hope that it is just a dream, or that we will wake up from this bad dream-like state, or that the Lord will come in a sweeping way to remove all of our distasteful emotions and bad feelings. We begin to start thinking that all the negative and ill feelings are temporary and bring God will get us back to the stable place in life that we knew before all of this unexpected death and sadness came crashing down in our lives.

REFLECTIONS

However, as nervous and uncertain thoughts begin to take us in and out of reality, some rational thinking begins to emerge and at some point, we start to reflect on the relationship we have with our Creator and our God. The rational mind begins to give way to His great Holy Spirit that nudges us and brings to our remembrance the precious scriptures that we have learned and lived …and so God's reassuring guidance begins to sink in.

We begin to recall passages in the *Book of Psalms*, bringing comfort from the only true, wise, and consoling God. He begins to comfort our souls with the remembrances of His holy word:

"Thou art my hiding place and my shield: I hope in thy word." – *Psalms 119:114*

"My soul melts for heaviness; strengthen me according to thy word." – *Psalms 119:28*

"In thee, oh Lord, do I hope." – *Psalms 38:15*

"Be of good courage, and He shall strengthen your heart." – *Psalms 31:24*

Impulsively, the heaviness of our burden starts turning as we remember to lean and depend on our mighty Creator, who knows our burdens and feels our every pain. We are reminded within ourselves to cast our broken hearts into the heart of our Lord and our God. We recognize in hazy unsteady hours of grief that He is indeed there with us. We cry out with more rivers of tears and anguish, while a myriad of thoughts and pictures flash through our mind's eye of the life of our dear loved one. We begin to fall into a clearer acknowledgement that he or she has taken the flight of transition from earth to God's glory.

＊＊＊

Death comes in its own time and in its own way. Time waits for no one, and death is no respecter of persons. All human flesh will experience the death and dying process; this is a fact for every living thing on the earth.

So, then we ask the question: Have we adequately prepared for this death "appointment" that we must keep?

Many times, in our Christian communities, families experiencing the loss of a family member or friend are not administratively prepared to function and execute the needful and necessary steps following the loss of the one they held dear. Then, as the rational thinking begins to creep into our minds, we realize the need to operate a little more effectively. Death visits our world in an instant. Family and friends begin to gather at the designated place to come together to mourn, discuss the deceased, and how to process and coordinate the required arrangements for burial or cremation. It is usually at this point where a designated lead family member begins to vocalize and start discussions centered around the following:

- How did they die? What was the exact cause of death?
- How is the spouse coping? How are the mom, dad, children, aunts, uncles, and other significant family members doing?

REFLECTIONS

✱ How soon did an emergency medical person arrive?

Reminiscing is an important way of processing a person's transition. It is important and cathartic to talk about the deceased's personality, how they lived their life, what they did at work, what they did at church, school, college or what community activities or clubs they were a part of.

Often, during this phase of grief, God sends the thoughtful human touch and ministering hands of help and hopefulness in this hour of great need. Unexpectedly, and without even realizing it, God may assign a person to help comfort and guide us through this hazy period of bereavement. This person suddenly appears and begins to gently and lovingly help us with daily tasks that we had completely forgotten existed. This calm, gentle person begins to fill us with comforting words while softly and intently beginning to manage the grief-stricken, as well as assuming the responsibility of helping us understand that we will get through this difficult time, one step and one day at a time.

The common, everyday tasks of sweeping the floor, vacuuming, washing dishes, preparing food, or even remembering to eat, drink, or feed your family are thoughtfully suggested and then often completed by this gifted, caring, helpful soul. The human touch of their hand on your shoulder, or the squeeze of your hand, and the softly whispered prayer to your ear are reassurances of hope that this season in your life will pass and you will go on to live productively. The ball of grief and bereavement weighs a ton at first, but the ministry of this helpful person allows the burden to feel just a bit lighter. We begin to rest with assurance that we will be victorious over this burden of loneliness, loss, and anxiety that accompanies this difficult time.

Slowly and intentionally, our minds begin to come around to the reality of all that has transpired with the death of our loved one. At some point a "click" snaps in our senses and we become aware of the planning to be done to make the required arrangements for burial, cremation, or funeral services.

We begin to recognize that the gifted ministerial person that God sent to our rescue has thoughtfully created a small list of tasks to assist us in performing activities that need to be done and completed within a small timeframe. We are grateful for this beginning effort and start to feel that the weight of our tasks that need to be completed is getting somewhat lighter. We are therefore ready to begin the challenge of assuming another level in our bereavement phase, which involves speaking with the hospital and facilities who have our loved one's remains and reaching out to a mortician.

How we reached this new point in our bereaved state, our finite minds cannot adequately comprehend. However, we have come to recognize that God's mercy and grace were in operation through the action of one of his beloved earthly angels.

A whirlwind of activities begins to unfold in our time of need. Our breathing no longer seems as suffocating as it felt a day or two ago. Our thoughts come to some sense of order regarding all that needs to be addressed with clarity and timing. We begin to experience an increase of faith as we recall again our knowledge of the Holy Scriptures.

"The just shall live by faith." - *Romans 1:17*.
"Without faith it is impossible to please God." - *Hebrews 11:6*.

After days of weeping and being out of touch with the reality of things around us, we have finally reached a small point of acceptance which allows us to move forward with organizing and planning all that must be done.

FINAL THOUGHTS

"Now I lay me down to sleep, I pray the Lord my soul to keep…" This children's prayer was written over a hundred years ago and we are still teaching and saying this prayer with our children at bedtime. But the sweet innocent prayer of a child on their knees is nothing compared to our thoughts and prayers when the actual death of someone occurs - whether they are young, old, or in an advanced state of illness. When the unexpected, untimely loss of a loved one happens, it is important to make time alone to mourn. Whether that includes crying, screaming, praying, or listening to music, this alone time is necessary to process the loss. And should this period of mourning continue past the point of what might be considered normal, grief counseling should be considered.

I am a firm believer of recommending that bereaved families seek out grief counseling. Oftentimes, we rationalize in our own minds that we are "OK," after a loved one has died. After the burial, cremation, and/or final phase of placing our loved one to rest, we convince ourselves that we will be fine to continue life without our loved one. However, studies indicate that it is during this time of aloneness, or when we find ourselves in the quiet of the house, after all the people

FINAL THOUGHTS

have gone and activities have ceased, that we can easily slip into uncontrollable anguish, fear, long-term loneliness, isolation and even depression. I personally found that there is nothing embarrassing or weak-minded about grief counseling for a man, a woman, or a child. In fact, participation in grief counseling activities, strengthen us, build us up, and bring us back to a sense of belonging, and increases our energy and faith. Depending on the type of counseling that is sought, we oftentimes can meet others in grief counseling who identify with all we are going through. We get to finally say things that we were afraid to say out loud to someone else. Grief counseling environments are a "non-judgement zone." I am here to testify that grief counseling activities are a breath of fresh air, a type of cleansing, a way to acknowledge that we are not alright, but it's ok, not to be alright, because we have to take the time to process through this season of our life and come to a clearer understanding of coping.

When the initial shock of a death wears off and you go about the planning of services and other final arrangements, keep a small notebook to date and write notes as you conduct all the business details. It is easy to forget what you did, or what needs to be done, since the grief may come in waves or when you least expect it.

Something critical that will need to be done or should be thought about now is estate planning. Estate planning is the process of establishing a framework to manage your assets upon death, disability, or incapacity. It involves creating documents that outline your specific wishes. While estate planning is not

FINAL THOUGHTS

a pleasant task, it is critical that a person implements it before they need it.

Now I lay me down to sleep,
I pray the Lord my Soul to keep.
If I should die before I wake,
I pray dear Lord, my Soul you'll take.

Mitchell, Sidney D. and Meyer, George W., "Now I Lay Me Down to Sleep" (1920).

~~~~~~~~~~~~~~~~~~~~

On the wings of death, the soul takes flight
The life we have lived, was but a vapor, now past from sight.
But if while on earth, we accepted the Master's Call,
We have, a prepared place, in His majestic halls.

DB Hudson

EPILOGUE

During the course of bringing this manuscript to closure, the world suffered a tragic and unimaginable loss when legendary basketball great, Kobe Bryant, age 41, and his precious 13-year-old daughter, Gianna, in addition to seven other parents, children, and the pilot were all killed in a helicopter crash outside of Calabasas, California on their way to their frequently attended basketball practice.

Our nation, the National Basketball Association (NBA), the Los Angeles Lakers, family members of all the other passengers on board, as well as millions of others around the globe, experienced uncontrollable heartbreak and devastation regarding this horrific news.

I could not let this moment pass without giving tribute to his legacy and memory, while also acknowledging and sending much love and prayers to his wife Vanessa, their other three daughters, and to his parents and siblings.

Just as importantly, I must take this time to reiterate that all I have been blessed to incorporate into this book clearly relates to the unfortunate, tragic, and untimely transition of what the Bryant family is now faced with having to experience. While

EPILOGUE

we mourn with the Bryant family, we also must learn from this tragedy that the death of our loved ones can come at the most unanticipated times in life. We must hug and love our children, husbands, wives, mothers, fathers, uncles, aunts, cousins, friends, and so many others, a little more tightly. We must honor and respect that making time to spend with one another, is a treasure that means more than running to work 2 to 3 jobs that keeps us from making memories with each other.

While we may think we are only taking a 10-minute ride to the pharmacy, grocery store, or allowing our kids to go to the playground, recreation center, or the local YMCA, let us remember that every second and every breath of life is precious. So, kiss and hug each time before parting company. Text to say you made it home okay. Time waits for no one. Stop putting off calling your parents, siblings, friends, or others that you may have had some disagreements with. While we want to live full and productive lives and make our giant footprint in the world, evilness, wickedness, or death could be lurking at any moment of the day. It is critical that we forgive immediately, show love, give smiles, and embrace one another a few extra times. Those other appointments on our iPhones and calendars can be rescheduled, or can just wait, as they pale in comparison to showing love and gratefulness toward one another.

MY APPEAL TO YOU, DEAR READER

When we ponder the question, "What is death?" or "What happens after death?" it is also important for us to consider the question, "What is life?" God has given mankind the wondrous gift of life. The Bible states that when God breathed "the breath of life" into Adam (*Genesis 2:7*), He gave the first human being more than just a physical existence. He imparted that spiritual and intellectual essence in Adam that gives us the remarkable capacities of the human mind. Therefore, because we have received these phenomenal gifts from God, mankind would do well to recognize that we are designed to live a productive life by honoring the Lord God with all He has bestowed into our beings.

Our lives should reflect a living love letter unto God, to give back to our Father God, a portion of the substance he has poured into us. After all, it is written, "Now we have received not the spirit of the world, but the Spirit that is from God, so that we may understand the gifts bestowed on us by God." (*1 Corinthians 2:12*). Spiritual understanding that surpasses our normal human intellect comes only through the extra help, influence and power that is derived of the Holy Spirit of God which was placed inside of us. Our human lives were created for higher heights in God. We were created with the expectation to do greater works upon the earth (*John 14:12*). Compared to plants and animals, humans were created by God with a spiritual dimension for a much higher purpose.

I have come to learn and know that the process of death is a part of the life that we breathe and live. Life is temporary. The Holy Scripture in the Book of James puts it this way: "You do not know what will happen tomorrow. For what is your life? It is but a vapor that appears for a little time then vanishes away." (*James 4:14*). The Lord Jesus Christ is the vehicle that God the Father sent for humans to receive salvation from their wicked, dark life and sin-laden souls.

I invite you and implore you to read and study the word of God for yourself, and to further examine these following scriptures on what we are to expect upon death, if we accept Jesus Christ as Lord and Savior over our soul. "For he that comes to God must believe that HE IS (i.e., that HE exists), and that he is a rewarder of them that diligently seek him." (*Hebrews 11:6*)

Death does not have to be the end of the matter, regarding everlasting life. *1 Corinthians 15:51* states, "Behold, I tell you a mystery: We shall not all sleep, but we shall all be changed." Here, the Apostle Paul uses the word "sleep" to describe a state of unconsciousness. According to *Hebrews 9:27*, our change will take place at the time of judgement, rather than at the moment of death. In the *Book of Job*, he declares "… if a man dies, shall he live again?" Then Job answers his own question, stating "… all the days of my appointed time and service, I will wait until my change comes." (*Job 14:14*)

The Scriptures point out that we are now mortal (or destructible), and that to receive everlasting life we must somehow become immortal (or indestructible). "… for this corruptible must put on incorruption, and this mortal must put on immortality. So when this corruptible has put on incorruption, and this mortal has put on immortality, then shall be bought to pass, the saying that is written: death is swallowed up in victory." (*1 Corinthians 15:53-54*)

Further, we are taught in *1 Thessalonians 4:13-14*, "I do not want you to be ignorant, brethren, concerning those who have fallen asleep, lest you sorrow as others who have no hope, for if we believe that Jesus died and rose again, even so God will bring with Him those who sleep in Jesus."

The prophet Daniel declares: "And many of them that sleep in the dust of the earth shall awake, some to everlasting life, and some to shame and everlasting contempt." (*Daniel 12:2*)

While we are among the living and breathing, we have the opportunity right now to seek out the understanding of salvation by accepting the Lord Jesus Christ as our savior. Because we do not know the time or hour of death (for example, Kobe Bryant), we should prepare to be in a state of "readiness." For our mortal, earthly man shall go back to the dust from where it came, and the spirit that is in man, which originally came from the Creator God, will return to Him. *Ecclesiastes 12:7* declares:" Then the dust will return to the earth as it was, and the spirit will return to God who gave it."

Learn to trust in the Lord with all your heart and lean not unto your own understanding (or intellect/mindset). "For our God so loved the world, that He gave His only begotten Son, that whoever should believe in Him will not perish, but will have everlasting life." (*John 3:16*) Therefore, when we accept Jesus Christ as Lord and Savior, we declare: "I am crucified with Christ: nevertheless I live; yet not I, but Christ lives in me, and the life which I now live in the flesh I live by the faith of the Son of God, who loved me, and gave himself for me." (*Galatians 2:20*)

Please receive this appeal that I am making to you. Your life is precious to our God. He is your maker and the lover of your soul. Through your belief in Him, death will be swallowed up in victory on your behalf. Just believe and trust God every step of the way. Make that life-changing decision today and get your life in order by accepting Christ as your Savior so that everlasting life after death can be your portion. He is calling your name!

RESOURCES

Listed below are several critical documents for you to learn about and understand what they are and how they protect your wishes and rights. I strongly recommend that you make time to have these documents drawn up while you are able to make your own decisions.

1. Last Will & Testament

The fundamental purpose of a will is to outline who will receive your assets upon your death. Another important purpose of a will is to specify guardianship for your minor children. A guardian is one who takes legal responsibility for the care of your minor or incapacitated children after you are gone. It is important to understand that a will does not become effective until the date of death. So, it does not provide any benefits during your lifetime. A will can be changed at any time (assuming you are not mentally incapacitated). It can be amended by using a codicil or revoked by writing a new will. A will can also create a trust upon your death. If your estate is large enough, you may also need to incorporate federal estate tax planning into your documents.

2. Trust

A trust is a legal instrument that provides ongoing management for your assets. It can be inter vivos (also known as a living trust, which exists during your lifetime) or testamentary (one that is created by your will upon your death). It is a good idea to leave assets in trust if the beneficiaries are minors, incapacitated, or if they are simply not fiscally responsible. The trust document names a trustee who has the responsibility of managing the assets in the trust and determines when and how much of the trust assets to distribute (subject to the terms you have written in the trust). You may want to name a trustee while your child is under a certain age, say 25 or 30. Then, once your child reaches that specific age, they can either act as their own trustee, or the trust can terminate and distribute all of the assets to your child outright.

3. Power of Attorney

A power of attorney allows you to empower someone else to act on your behalf for legal and financial decisions. It can be a durable power of attorney, which becomes effective immediately, or a springing power of attorney, which becomes effective upon a stipulated event, typically when you are disabled or mentally incompetent. It is critical that you completely trust the person to whom you provide this power, as he or she can legally act on your behalf.

4. Healthcare Power of Attorney (also known as Advanced Healthcare Directive)

A healthcare power of attorney (also known as a medical power of attorney) gives a trusted individual the authority to make decisions about your medical treatment should you be unable to do so on your own. No financial authority is granted in this document, only medical power. So, you could provide one person the durable power of attorney and another person the healthcare power of attorney if you desire.

5. Living Will or Last Will and Testament

While the healthcare power of attorney authorizes another to make medical decisions on your behalf, a living will (also known as a directive to physicians), sets out your predetermined wishes regarding end-of-life care should you become terminally ill or permanently unconscious. Essentially, it takes the decision to withhold life out of the hands of your medical providers and the ones you love so that they are not burdened by it, and so that you can be assured your wishes are respected.

6. HIPAA Release

One of the important provisions of the Health Insurance Portability and Accountability Act of 1996 (HIPAA) is the obligation that medical records be kept confidential. While this is an important requirement, it can have severe unintended consequences. Without the legal authority to share medical records, your family may not be able to obtain important information regarding your medical condition and treatment if you were to become incapacitated. A HIPAA release allows your medical providers to share and discuss your medical situation with whomever you specify in the document.

7. Letter of Intent

A letter of intent is a simple, nonbinding personal letter to the ones you love expressing your desires and special requests. It may include information regarding burial or cremation, or a specific bequest of collectibles or personal items. While it does not typically have legal authority, it can help to clear up confusion to the ones you leave behind regarding how you would like your personal preferences to be executed.

The list I have developed below is in no specific order but may apply to your circumstance or situation at the death of a loved one or friend.

1. Make sure to locate important papers, including last wishes communicated by your deceased loved one.
- Obtain Social Security card or number.
- If loved one was in the military, immediately start the process of obtaining a copy of their DD214 (military separation document and proof of military service).
- Obtain bank account information (particularly if direct deposit is from SSA or a pension agency).
- List of bills that need to be paid or settled.
- Online passwords, passwords to computers, iPads, phones, tablets, and all electronic devices.

- ✧ Keys to safe and/or location of safe deposit boxes.
- ✧ Video or recordings of loved one's last words and directions.

2. *Planning the Funeral/Burial*
- ✧ Meet with the Pastor, Minister, Rabbi, etc. to discuss use of the church, synagogue, or other facility, to determine dates and availability for your intended service times.
- ✧ Discuss the intended program and the type of activities you would like to incorporate of other entities you would like to invite, i.e. military groups, organizations like the Masons, Eastern Stars, Fraternities,
- ✧ Discuss cost, bathrooms, acceptance of flower arrangements, etc.

3. *Visiting/Interviewing Morticians*
- ✧ Go to more than one mortician. I suggest going to at least three. Remember, they are businesses. Just as with any business, compare the products and services they offer and money you are expected to pay. Look at the quality of items you will get for your budgeted dollar. You do not have to spend every cent of the insurance policy with the undertaker. Remember, you will still need to have money for living expenses after you have buried your loved one.
- ✧ If you have a loved one already in hospice or in the process of transitioning, try to manage your grief state so you can make time to visit the morticians before the transition crossover of your loved one. This will save some time later regarding tasks and burdensome activities that

the family may have to handle in the days to come. The things you are able to accomplish while your loved one is in hospice care will then be something you can check off on your list of things to do.

4. *Identification of Legal Documents- (Make sure while your loved one was living they discussed the location of their legal documents)*

- Make sure you locate and keep these documents throughout the process of conducting business for the deceased.
- Make sure you think of HOW MANY death certificates you will need. Have the undertaker help you purchase them when they retrieve the remains of your loved one. It can be difficult to obtain death certificates at a later date down the road.
- Military Separation Papers are extremely important. Keep copies of the deceased DD214 when conducting business. Be cautious of who you release them over to.
- Last Will and Testament
- Power of Attorney (POA
- Health Care Directive, Living Will

5. *Discussion of Advanced Care Directive*

- Who is authorized on the advanced care directive? This is very important information to be aware of, particularly when the loved one is going through a lengthy illness or is in Hospice Care.
- Discussion/Preparation of Power of Attorney and Will (Imperative)

- ✧ If a POA or will does not exist for yourself or your loved ones, PLEASE GET ONE IN PLACE NOW! These are critical documents for financial and fiduciary interests of the deceased. If there is not one in place, NO ONE will be able to act on behalf of the deceased's businesses, trusts, bank accounts, closing out social media, or any financial matter that they acquired or were involved in during life.
- ✧ If one is in place, find out who is listed as POA and executor of the deceased's estate.

7. Estate Planning/Legal Counsel

8. Bank Accounts/Available or Hidden Cash Assets
- ✧ Bank card pin numbers.
- ✧ Name of bank (along with checking or saving account numbers).

9. Identification of Clergy, Pastors, Ministers, Rabbi, Muslim Leader
- ✧ You must make time to call and arrange discussion/meetings with these individuals. Their schedules are busy, and they could be out of town or out of the country. Find out who their administrator or secretary is early on; they are usually the one who has the calendar of the clergy or minister.

10. Location (City and State) of Deceased's Remains
- ✧ Find out associated costs for shipping the remains.

✧ Find out phone numbers and contact the hospital, morgue or police department morgue where the deceased's remains are located. Find out how long the body can stay in their facility. GET NAMES and PHONE NUMBERS of all persons in charge that you may speak with (remember the little notebook that I mentioned earlier—you need this for making important notes and dates).

11. Location of Insurance Policies
✧ Please note who the beneficiary is on any insurance policies.

12. *If loved one was a business owner, locate proprietary paperwork and check for any partnerships with the business.*

13. *Marriage Certificates and/or Divorce Papers*

14. *Legal Adoption Papers for Children*

15. *Obituary Preparation* – It is best to have a confidante and person you trust to help you prepare this document. Research typesetting services and professional printers for associated costs.

16. *Bereavement Counseling (This is so important to pursue)*

Remember, you are grieving and there is a myriad of emotions that you are going through during the bereavement process. Make sure you have someone that you can trust and lean on as you make critical decisions during this painful time. Emotions have a way of distracting us and preventing us from making rational decisions regarding life and business choices. Having a confident, trustworthy, rationally-minded person in your corner can really help you with sorting things out during this time. I recognize the importance of this role, as I have been that designated person to so many. And it is not mandatory that it be a family member, but rather someone you know and trust to carry out your wishes.

It is also important to remember to WRITE DOWN notes on all activities, business transactions, and decisions that are being made during your bereavement process. We are all human and therefore subject to forget things, especially during times of stress. Take the time to keep and carry that small notebook in your purse or pocket so that you can make notations and then refer back to it at any given time. Remember to place in your entries, the date/time, and name of persons you spoke to about the business matter or choices made, along with needed contact information.

Morticians/Funeral Homes

- When interviewing them, look for compassionate, caring, professional persons.
- Discuss where to obtain the remains of the loved one, particularly if the remains are in a police or hospital morgue that is located in another state.
- Take time to discuss costs and insurance policies. Make sure you have a clear understanding of the process. (Again, write things down).
- Examine their facilities closely. Know the exact location and room where your funeral or memorial service will take place.

Preparation of a Written Obituary
- Gather pictures and keep them all in one safe place/location.
- Remember to acknowledge printing and paper costs.
- Inquire about typesetting and template costs.
- Gather life accomplishments information about the deceased loved one. Collect resume, information from family, friends, co-workers, community folks, memberships of organizations, etc.
- Examine associated costs for florists/flowers.
- Organizing Funeral or Memorial Services at a church:
  - Meet with pastors/churches/ministers.
  - Look at accessibility of the church/synagogue/building
    - For determining suitability
    - For handicapped persons
    - Stairs/elevators/lift accommodations for maneuvering of a casket with different body types and sizes

Timing and Coordination of All Activities
- Communication between church staff and selected mortician staff is a must. Make sure it happens.
- Determine time and day of arrangements and get them communicated out to newspaper, Facebook, social media, community flyer, etc.
- Be mindful of the time needed to process anything through the U.S. Armed forces, if deceased loved one

was a veteran or was actively on duty with military, or if deceased loved one was a member of a police department, fire department, or any type of emergency response organization. Different protocols are to be considered if engaging these types of associations. Become knowledgeable with requirements for burial sites, if deceased loved one will be laid to rest within the protocols of these types of organizations.

* Listen effectively to become knowledgeable about pricing for executing a funeral or memorial service. Every little "extra" item a family may want to have incorporated into the final arrangements will probably carry with it an additional incurrence of cost.

* Examine weekend versus weekday associated costs along with daytime versus nighttime service or memorial arrangement.

* Always ask and identify who will incur what costs. U.S. Armed forces, U.S. Veteran Affairs, Fraternal Order of Police, firefighters, emergency responders, etc. usually take on the responsibility of absorbing burial costs if the deceased loved one was a part of one of these organizations. Remember to ask and write it down.

* Explore donating the body to science if this is something that your deceased loved one wanted. Have someone research for you exactly how that process is executed.

* If you and your family elect cremation services, research the process and cost for this.

While I have tried to mention many resources that I think individuals may want or need to pursue, my listings are not conclusive. You may think of something else you and your family/friends need to consider. Keep this guidebook with you to refer to and to take notes. (This is why I have a section at the back of this book for notetaking.)

I have a passion for this ministry work and therefore I will not cease to pray for all who must go through experiencing the loss of someone they hold dear. Remember to trust God, be at peace, and get rest for the strength you will need during this season of your life. You are still among the land of the living, so remember that this too shall pass, and you will have joy and celebration in your life again.

REFERENCES

Book References
- References to Biblical Holy Scripture and all quoted scriptures are from:
  - *Thomas Nelson New King James Version of the Bible*
  - *Life Application Bible*
  - *Amplified Version of the Bible*
  - *Christian Standard Bible*
- Jimmy Swaggart's *The Expositor's Bible Study, King James Version*
- *Gone From My Sight – the Dying Experience* by Barbara Karnes, RN
- *What Happens After Death?* – International Association of the United Church of God, 2004
- *On Death and Dying* – Elizabeth Kubler Ross, 1969

Website References
- *www.Burialplanning.com* (tips on burial planning to consider)

- *www.Legalzoom.com* (legal guidance and help on wills and POAs)
- *www.nia.nih.gov/health/advance-care-planning-healthcare-directives*
- *www.nia.nih.gov/health/getting-your-affairs-order*
- *www.achaheart.org* (advance care health directives)
- *www.activebeat.com/your-health/6-tips-to-help-you-through-the-grieving-process*
- *www.hospicecare.org/education/death-and-dying* (quality of life for loved ones)
- *www.stjude.org* (St Jude Children's Research Hospital for children with cancer)

Note: I am not endorsing one or the other. And I do not guarantee that these websites are still functioning as listed as vendors choose to change or update names of their websites at any given time.

Suggested Insurance Companies *(that provide whole life insurance)*

Note: I am not endorsing one or the other. And I do not guarantee that these websites are still functioning as listed as vendors choose to change or update names of their websites at any given time.

- Allstate – *www.allstate.com*
- Colonial Penn – *www.colonialpenn.com*
- Fidelity – *www.fidelitylife.com*

- Globe Life – *www.globelifeinsurance.com*
- Lincoln Financial – *www.lfg.com*
- Mass Mutual – *www.massmutual.com*
- Mutual of Omaha – *www.mutualofomaha.com*
- New York Life – *www.newyorklife.com*
- Texas Life – *www.texaslife.com*
- Transamerica – *www.transamerica.com*

NOTES